I0017207

CYBER

KIDS

Learn how to keep your kids safe in the cyber world we live in today. By continuing the conversation and staying committed to cyber awareness, we can empower our children and teens to make responsible choices, navigate the digital world safely, and become confident digital citizens.

MARK HUGHES

TABLE OF CONTENTS

CHAPTER 1:
INTRODUCTION

The Importance of Cyber Awareness in Today's Digital Age

In today's digital age, where technology plays a crucial role in our daily lives, it is more important than ever to raise cyber-aware kids. As parents, educators, schools, and teachers, we play a significant role in fostering a safe and responsible digital environment for our children and teens.

Cyber awareness refers to the knowledge and understanding of potential risks, threats, and appropriate behaviors in the online world. It encompasses various aspects, including online privacy, digital footprints, cyberbullying, online predators, and the responsible use of technology. By instilling cyber awareness in our young ones, we empower them to navigate the digital landscape confidently while minimizing the risks associated with it.

One of the primary reasons why cyber awareness is crucial is the ever-evolving nature of technology. With new social media platforms, apps, and online games emerging constantly, it becomes essential for parents, educators, schools, and teachers to stay informed and up-to-date. By doing so, we can guide our children and teens to make informed decisions, recognize potential dangers, and protect themselves online.

Another critical aspect of cyber awareness is the prevention of cyberbullying. Unfortunately, cyberbullying has become a prevalent issue in recent years, causing immense harm to young individuals. By educating children and teens about the consequences of cyberbullying, teaching them empathy, and fostering a culture of respect, we can contribute to creating a safer online environment.

Furthermore, cyber awareness helps children and teens understand the importance of safeguarding their personal information online. By teaching them about privacy settings, the risks of sharing sensitive information, and the significance of strong passwords, we empower them to protect themselves from potential harm.

Additionally, cyber awareness encourages responsible digital citizenship. It encompasses teaching children and teens about proper online etiquette, promoting critical thinking skills, and encouraging them to be responsible for their actions online. By nurturing these qualities, we raise a generation of responsible digital citizens who can contribute positively to the online community.

In conclusion, cyber awareness plays a vital role in today's digital age. As parents, educators, schools, and teachers, it is our responsibility to equip our children and teens with the necessary knowledge and skills to navigate the online world safely and responsibly. By doing so, we can ensure that they make informed decisions, protect themselves from potential risks, and contribute positively to the digital community. Together, let us go beyond the screen and raise cyber-aware kids who are prepared for the challenges and opportunities of the digital age.

UNDERSTANDING THE RISKS AND DANGERS OF THE ONLINE WORLD

In today's digital age, it is crucial for parents, educators, schools, and teachers to be well- informed about the risks and dangers that exist in the online world. With children and teenagers spending an increasing amount of
time online, it is essential to provide them with the necessary tools and knowledge to navigate the digital landscape safely. This chapter aims to shed light on the potential threats children and teens may encounter online and the importance of cyber awareness.

One of the primary risks in the online world is cyberbullying. With the anonymity that the internet provides, bullies can target victims with relentless and harmful messages, leading to severe emotional and psychological distress. Parents and educators must be aware of the signs of cyberbullying and take immediate action to protect their children from such harmful behavior.

Another significant danger is the risk of online predators. These individuals often disguise themselves as trustworthy individuals to gain the trust of children and teens. They may engage in grooming behaviors, leading to potential ofline encounters that can have devastating consequences. By understanding how predators operate and teaching children about the importance of online privacy and skepticism, parents and educators can help safeguard their children against these threats.

Furthermore, the online world poses risks related to inappropriate content. Children and teens may stumble upon explicit or violent material that can negatively impact their emotional and psychological well-being. It is crucial for adults to implement filters and monitoring tools to limit exposure to such content and engage in open conversations with children about appropriate online behavior.

Additionally, the issue of online scams and identity theft cannot be ignored. Children and teens are often not fully aware of the potential risks of sharing personal information online, making them ideal targets for scammers.
Educating children about the importance of protecting personal information and recognizing online scams is vital in safeguarding their online presence.

Overall, understanding the risks and dangers of the online world is of paramount importance in raising cyber-aware kids. By equipping parents, educators, schools, and teachers with the knowledge and resources to address these risks, we can create a safer digital environment for children and teens.

Through proactive measures such as open communication, monitoring, and education, we can empower our children to make responsible decisions online and navigate the digital landscape with confidence and resilience.

THE ROLE OF PARENTS, EDUCATORS, SCHOOLS, AND TEACHERS IN RAISING CYBER-AWARE KIDS

In today's digital age, where children and teens are constantly connected to screens, it is crucial for parents, educators, schools, and teachers to play an active role in raising cyber- aware kids. With the ever-increasing cyber threats and the potential dangers lurking online, it has become imperative to equip our children with the knowledge and skills to navigate the digital world safely. Parents are the first line of defense when it comes to raising cyber-aware kids. They have the responsibility to educate their children about the potential risks online and to establish rules and boundaries for internet usage. By fostering open communication and maintaining an ongoing dialogue with their children, parents can create a safe and supportive environment where kids feel comfortable discussing their online experiences and seeking guidance when needed.

Educators and schools also play a crucial role in raising cyber-aware kids. By incorporating cyber safety into the curriculum, schools can provide students with the necessary knowledge and skills to navigate the digital landscape responsibly. Educators can teach students about online privacy, the importance of strong passwords, and how to identify and respond to cyberbullying. By fostering a culture of digital responsibility within the school community, educators can help create a safe and inclusive online environment for students.

Teachers have a unique opportunity to influence and guide their students in the digital realm. By staying informed about the latest online trends and threats, teachers can provide valuable insights and advice to their students. They can also promote critical thinking skills and digital literacy, empowering students to evaluate the credibility of online information and make informed decisions.Teachers can act as positive rolemodels, demonstrating responsible online behavior and teaching students about the ethical use of technology.

Overall, the collective efforts of parents, educators, schools, and teachers are crucial in raising cyber-aware kids. By working together, we can create a safe and supportive digital environment for children and teens. It is essential that we equip our children with the necessary knowledge and skills to navigate the online world responsibly and confidently. By doing so, we can ensure that they develop into responsible digital citizens who understand the potential risks and make informed decisions online.

CHAPTER 2: BUILDING A STRONG FOUNDATION

Setting Boundaries and Establishing Digital Guidelines

In today's digital age, it is crucial for parents, educators, schools, and teachers to take an active role in raising cyber-aware kids. With the vast array of online platforms and the increasing accessibility of technology, setting boundaries and establishing digital guidelines have become more important than ever before.

One of the first steps in creating a safe digital environment for children and teens is setting clear boundaries. Establishing limits on screen time can help prevent excessive use and

promote a healthy balance between online and ofline activities. Parents and educators should collaborate to create a schedule that allows for ample time for physical exercise, socializing, and other non-digital activities. By setting these boundaries early on, children will develop a better understanding of the value of time and the importance of moderation.

In addition to time constraints, it is vital to establish guidelines regarding the types of content children are exposed to online.

Parents and educators should educate themselves about age-appropriate material and ensure that children are accessing websites, apps, and games that align with their developmental stage. Regularly monitoring online activities and engaging in open conversations about potential risks and dangers will empower children to make responsible choices while navigating the digital world.

Another essential aspect of setting boundaries involves privacy and personal information.
Children and teens must understand the significance of protecting their online identities and the potential consequences of oversharing. Parents, educators, schools, and teachers should encourage their young ones to maintain strict privacy settings, avoid sharing personal details, and think twice before accepting friend requests or engaging in conversations with strangers.
Lastly, it is crucial to establish guidelines on online etiquette and digital citizenship.
Children should be taught the importance of respectful and responsible behavior online, including refraining from cyberbullying, sharing inappropriate content, or engaging in harmful activities. Encouraging empathy, kindness, and critical thinking will help children develop strong ethical values online.

By setting boundaries and establishing digital guidelines, parents, educators, schools, and teachers can ensure that children and teens become cyber-aware individuals. It is essential to remember that these guidelines should be flexible, adapting to the ever-evolving digital landscape. By nurturing a supportive and open environment, we can empower the next generation to harness the benefits of technology while navigating the potential risks responsibly.

TEACHING ONLINE ETIQUETTE AND RESPONSIBLE DIGITAL CITIZENSHIP

In today's digital age, where children and teenagers spend a significant amount of their time online, it is crucial for parents, educators, schools, and teachers to prioritize teaching online etiquette and responsible digital citizenship. As the world becomes increasingly interconnected, it is important to raise cyber-aware kids who understand the implications of their digital actions and can navigate the online world safely and responsibly.

Online etiquette refers to the set of rules and norms that govern behavior in the digital realm. Just as we teach our children to be polite, respectful, and considerate in face-to- face interactions, we must impart these values in their online interactions as well. Teaching online etiquette involves educating children about the importance of being respectful, kind, and empathetic towards others online.

This includes refraining from cyberbullying, spreading rumors, or engaging in any form of harmful behavior. By promoting positive online behavior, we can create a safer and more inclusive digital environment for all.

Responsible digital citizenship goes beyond etiquette and encompasses a broader understanding of the digital landscape. It involves teaching children about the potential risks and consequences of their online actions, such as the permanence of digital footprints and the importance of protecting their personal information. Educators and parents should guide children on how to identify and avoid scams, phishing attempts, and malicious websites. They should also emphasize the need to critically evaluate online information and be mindful of the impact of their online presence on their future opportunities.

To effectively teach online etiquette and responsible digital citizenship, parents, educators, schools, and teachers can employ various strategies. These may include integrating digital literacy education into the curriculum, organizing workshops and seminars, and using interactive resources that promote engagement and understanding. It is also essential to maintain open lines of communication with children and teenagers, creating a safe space where they can share their online experiences and seek guidance when faced with challenging situations.

By prioritizing the teaching of online etiquette and responsible digital citizenship, we can equip our children and teenagers with the necessary skills and knowledge to navigate the digital world safely and responsibly.
Together, let us empower the next generation to become responsible digital citizens who can thrive in the interconnected world beyond the screen.

DEVELOPING CRITICAL THINKING AND MEDIA LITERACY SKILLS

In this ever-evolving digital age, it is crucial for parents, educators, schools, and teachers to equip children and teens with the necessary skills to navigate the vast and sometimes treacherous landscape of the online world.

One of the most essential skills to impart to young individuals is critical thinking and media literacy.

Critical thinking enables children and teens to analyze and evaluate information, enabling them to make informed decisions and form their own opinions. In a world saturated with information, it is becoming increasingly important to teach young individuals how to critically assess the credibility and reliability of the sources they encounter online. By developing critical thinking skills, children and teens will be better equipped to distinguish between fact and fiction, recognize bias, and identify persuasive techniques employed by various media platforms.

Media literacy, on the other hand, focuses on empowering children and teens to become active and discerning participants in the digital world. By teaching media literacy, parents, educators, schools, and teachers can help young individuals develop a critical awareness of the media's influence and its role in shaping opinions and beliefs. This skill enables children and teens to question, deconstruct, and analyze media messages, ensuring that they are not blindly influenced by potentially harmful or misleading content.

To foster critical thinking and media literacy skills in children and teens, it is crucial to integrate these concepts into their education. Educators and teachers should create opportunities for students to engage in discussions and debates, encouraging them to express their opinions and challenge each other's ideas. Schools should also incorporate media literacy into the curriculum, providing students with the tools to critically analyze media messages and encouraging them to create their own media content.

Parents can play a significant role in developing critical thinking and media literacy skills by engaging in open and honest discussions with their children about the online world. By encouraging children to question the information they encounter and discussing the potential biases and motives behind media messages, parents can help their children develop a healthy skepticism and an ability to think critically about the information they consume.

In conclusion, developing critical thinking and media literacy skills is crucial in raising cyber- aware kids in a digital age. By equipping children and teens with these skills, parents, educators, schools, and teachers can empower young individuals to navigate the online world safely, make informed decisions, and become active participants in shaping their digital experiences.

CHAPTER 3: NURTURING SAFE ONLINE RELATIONSHIPS

Teaching Children about Online Predators and Stranger Danger

In today's digital age, it is crucial for parents, educators, schools, and teachers to equip children with the knowledge and skills to navigate the online world safely. With the increasing presence of online predators and the potential dangers lurking behind screens, it is essential to address the topic of online predators and stranger danger with children. This subchapter aims to provide valuable insights and practical strategies for teaching children about these risks, ensuring their cyber awareness and safety.

One of the primary goals is to help children understand who online predators are and how they operate. Educators and parents can start by explaining that online predators are individuals who use the internet to manipulate, exploit, and harm children. It is crucial to emphasize that these predators may pretend to be someone they are not, hiding behind fake profiles, and often target vulnerable children.

To teach children about stranger danger in the online world, it is essential to encourage open communication. Parents and educators should create a safe and non-judgmental environment where children can freely discuss their online experiences, concerns, and potential encounters. By fostering trust and understanding, children will feel more comfortable sharing any unusual or uncomfortable interactions they have had online.

In addition, teaching children about the warning signs of online predators is vital. These signs may include someone asking for personal information, attempting to meet in person, or requesting explicit photos. By educating children about these red lags, they can quickly identify and report any suspicious online behavior.

Furthermore, it is crucial to educate children about setting boundaries and maintaining privacy online. Children should be taught to avoid sharing personal information, such as their full name, address, phone number, or school, with anyone they meet online. Emphasizing the importance of privacy settings and the need to keep personal information private is essential for their online safety.

To reinforce these lessons, educators and parents should incorporate interactive activities and discussions into their curriculum or family routines. Engaging children in role- playing scenarios, where they practice how to respond to potential online predators, can be especially helpful. Additionally, providing real-life examples and stories of children who have encountered online predators can effectively illustrate the dangers and consequences.

Teaching children about online predators and stranger danger is an ongoing process that requires consistent reinforcement. As technology continues to evolve, parents, educators, schools, and teachers must remain vigilant, adapting their strategies to address the ever-changing landscape of the digital world. By equipping children with the knowledge, skills, and confidence to navigate the online world safely, we can empower them to become responsible digital citizens and protect themselves from potential harm.

BUILDING TRUST AND OPEN COMMUNICATION IN THE DIGITAL SPACE

In today's digital age, where children and teens are increasingly connected to the online world, it is crucial for parents, educators, schools, and teachers to prioritize building trust and open communication with them.

The rapid evolution of technology and the ever-expanding reach of the internet have presented new challenges and risks that can impact cyber awareness for children and teens. By fostering trust and open communication, we can empower them to navigate the digital space safely and responsibly.

Trust serves as the foundation for any meaningful relationship, and it is no different in the digital realm. Parents and educators must establish trust with their children and students by creating an environment where they feel comfortable sharing their online experiences, concerns, and questions. This trust can be built by engaging in open, non- judgmental conversations about the digital world and genuinely listening to their perspectives. By doing so, parents and educators can gain valuable insights into the challenges children and teens face online and provide appropriate guidance and support.

Open communication is equally important in the digital space. Parents and educators should encourage children and teens to speak openly about their online activities, friends, and any issues they encounter. By actively listening and maintaining an open dialogue, adults can identify potential risks or harmful situations and address them promptly. It is crucial to create a space where children and teens feel comfortable sharing their experiences without fear of punishment or dismissal. This open communication can also help parents and educators stay updated on the latest trends, apps, and platforms, enabling them to provide relevant guidance and ensure cyber awareness.

To foster trust and open communication, it is essential to lead by example. Parents and educators should demonstrate responsible online behavior, such as respecting privacy, avoiding cyberbullying, and being mindful of the content they share. By modeling positive digital habits, adults can set a standard for children and teens to follow. Additionally, parents and educators should stay informed about digital safety strategies, privacy settings, and parental control tools to better guide their children and students in navigating the digital space.

In conclusion, building trust and open communication in the digital space is crucial for promoting cyber awareness among children and teens. By establishing trust, encouraging open dialogue, and leading by example, parents, educators, schools, and teachers can empower young individuals to make informed decisions, navigate the digital world safely, and become responsible digital citizens.

RECOGNIZING AND RESPONDING TO CYBERBULLYING

In today's digital age, where children and teens are constantly connected to the internet, cyberbullying has become a prevalent issue. It is crucial for parents, educators, schools, and teachers to be aware of this problem and equip themselves with the knowledge and tools to recognize and respond effectively to cyberbullying incidents. This subchapter aims to provide valuable insights and practical strategies to address cyberbullying in a way that promotes cyber awareness for children and teens.

Recognizing cyberbullying is the first step towards combating it. Parents, educators, schools, and teachers should familiarize themselves with the various forms of cyberbullying, such as online harassment, spreading rumors or gossip, impersonation, and exclusion. By understanding these tactics, they can better identify when a child or teen is being targeted. It is important to maintain open lines of communication with children and teens, encouraging them to share their online experiences without fear of judgment or punishment.

Once cyberbullying has been identified, a swift and appropriate response is essential. Parents should provide emotional support to their child or teen, assuring them that they are not alone and that their feelings are valid.

Educators, schools, and teachers should have clear protocols in place to address cyberbullying incidents, involving parents and other relevant stakeholders. It is crucial to document incidents, collect evidence, and report them to the appropriate authorities or social media platforms.

Prevention plays a crucial role in combating cyberbullying. Parents, educators, schools, and teachers should educate children and teens about responsible online behavior, emphasizing the importance of empathy, respect, and digital citizenship. Encouraging children and teens to think critically about their online actions and the impact they may have on others can help prevent cyberbullying incidents from occurring in the first place.

Creating a supportive and safe online environment is also vital. Parents should consider using parental control software and monitoring their children's online activities without invading their privacy. Educators, schools, and teachers should promote a culture of inclusivity and understanding, fostering an atmosphere where students feel comfortable reporting cyberbullying incidents.

In conclusion, recognizing and responding to cyberbullying is crucial for parents, educators, schools, and teachers. By understanding the various forms of cyberbullying and responding appropriately, we can protect our children and teens from the harmful effects of online harassment. Prevention and education are key in empowering children and teens to navigate the digital world responsibly. By working together, we can raise cyber-aware kids who are equipped to handle cyberbullying and create a safer online environment for all.

CHAPTER 4: PROTECTING PERSONAL INFORMATION

Understanding the Importance of Privacy Settings and Security Measures

In today's digital age, where children and teens spend a significant amount of time online, it is crucial for parents, educators, schools, and teachers to understand the importance of privacy settings and security measures. With cyber threats and online dangers becoming increasingly prevalent, it is essential to equip children with the knowledge and tools to navigate the virtual world safely.

Privacy settings are vital in protecting personal information and ensuring that online activities remain private. By utilizing privacy settings on social media platforms, websites, and applications, parents can help control what information is shared and who has access to it. Educators and schools can also play a significant role in teaching children about the importance of privacy settings and how to set them up effectively.

Privacy settings allow users to manage their online presence, control who can view their profiles, and limit the amount of personal information that is accessible. They provide an additional layer of protection against potential cyber threats, such as identity theft, cyberbullying, and online scams. By understanding and utilizing privacy settings, parents, educators, schools, and teachers can empower children to take control of their online presence and protect themselves from harm.

Alongside privacy settings, security measures are equally important in safeguarding children online. Educators and schools should educate children about the significance of strong and unique passwords, the dangers of sharing passwords with others, and the importance of keeping their devices secure. By teaching children about the potential risks of downloading malicious software or clicking on suspicious links, educators can help them develop good digital hygiene habits.

Furthermore, parents, educators, schools, and teachers should stay up-to-date with the latest security measures and technologies.
This includes understanding the importance of antivirus software, firewalls, and secure browsing habits. By staying informed, they can provide children with the necessary guidance and support to navigate the online world securely.

In conclusion, understanding the importance of privacy settings and security measures is crucial for parents, educators, schools, and teachers in raising cyber-aware kids. By empowering children with the knowledge and tools to protect their online presence, we can help them navigate the digital landscape safely. By prioritizing privacy settings and security measures, we can ensure that our children and teens are equipped to face the challenges of the digital age confidently.

EDUCATING CHILDREN ABOUT THE RISKS OF SHARING PERSONAL INFORMATION ONLINE

In today's digital age, where children and teens are constantly connected to the online world, it has become more crucial than ever to educate them about the risks associated with sharing personal information online. As parents, educators, schools, and teachers, it is our responsibility to equip the younger generation with the necessary knowledge and skills to navigate the digital landscape safely.

The internet offers countless opportunities for learning, socializing, and exploring new interests. However, it also poses significant risks, such as identity theft, cyberbullying, and online predators. By educating children about these risks, we can empower them to make informed decisions and protect themselves online.

One of the first steps in educating children about the risks of sharing personal information online is to teach them the importance of privacy. Children need to understand that personal information, such as
their full name, address, phone number, and even photographs, should not be shared with strangers or on public platforms. They should be encouraged to think critically before sharing any

information and consider the potential consequences.

Another crucial aspect of educating children about online risks is teaching them about the permanence of digital footprints. Once information is shared online, it can be difficult, if not impossible, to completely erase it.
Children need to be aware that their online actions can have long-term consequences and may impact their future opportunities, such as college admissions or job prospects.

Parents, educators, schools, and teachers can also guide children in understanding the concept of digital citizenship. This includes teaching them about responsible online behavior, empathy, and respect for others. By promoting positive digital interactions, we can help prevent cyberbullying and encourage a safe and inclusive online environment.

Furthermore, it is essential to keep an open line of communication with children and encourage them to share any concerns or incidents they encounter online. By fostering a safe and non-judgmental environment, children will feel more comfortable seeking guidance when faced with risky situations.

In conclusion, educating children about the risks of sharing personal information online is of utmost importance in today's digital age. Parents, educators, schools, and teachers play a vital role in equipping children with the necessary knowledge and skills to navigate the online world safely. By teaching them about privacy, the permanence of digital footprints, responsible online behavior, and fostering open communication, we can raise cyber- aware kids who are capable of making informed decisions and protecting themselves online.

TEACHING STRATEGIES FOR SAFELY MANAGING ONLINE ACCOUNTS AND PASSWORDS

In today's digital age, where children and teenagers are increasingly active online, it is crucial for parents, educators, and schools to teach effective strategies for safely managing online accounts and passwords. By instilling cyber awareness in our children, we can ensure their online safety and protect them from potential cyber threats.

One of the first steps in teaching children about online account and password management is to emphasize the importance of strong and unique passwords. Encourage them to create passwords that are not easily guessable, using a combination of letters, numbers, and symbols. Emphasize the need for a different password for each online account, as using the same password across multiple platforms can lead to disastrous consequences if one account is compromised.

Another teaching strategy is to educate children about the dangers of sharing passwords with friends or strangers.

Emphasize that passwords are private and should never be shared, even with their closest friends. Teach them about the potential risks, such as identity theft or unauthorized access to personal information, that can result from sharing passwords.

Additionally, it is crucial to teach children about the importance of regularly updating their passwords. Encourage them to change their passwords every few months or whenever they suspect any suspicious activity on their accounts. This practice can help prevent unauthorized access and maintain their online security.

Furthermore, parents, educators, and schools should emphasize the significance of two- factor authentication (2FA) as an additional layer of security. Teach children about the benefits of enabling 2FA, which requires a second form of verification, such as a unique code sent to their mobile device, in addition to their password. This extra step can significantly reduce the risk of unauthorized access to their accounts.

Lastly, it is important to teach children about the importance of being vigilant and recognizing phishing attempts. Phishing is a common tactic used by cybercriminals to trick individuals into revealing their login credentials. Teach children to verify the authenticity of emails, messages, or links before clicking on them, and to report any suspicious activity to a trusted adult.

By implementing these teaching strategies, parents, educators, and schools can equip children and teenagers with the necessary knowledge and skills to safely manage their online accounts and passwords. Empowering them with cyber awareness will not only protect them from potential cyber threats but also help them become responsible digital citizens in the ever-evolving digital landscape.

CHAPTER 5: PREVENTING ONLINE EXPLOITATION AND SCAMS

Identifying and Avoiding Online Scams, Phishing, and Malware
In today's digital age, where children and teens are spending more time online than ever before, it is crucial for parents, educators, schools, and teachers to equip themselves with the knowledge and tools to raise cyber- aware kids. One of the most significant threats lurking on the internet is the presence of online scams, phishing attempts, and malware. In this subchapter, we will explore the importance of identifying and avoiding these threats to ensure the safety and well- being of our children.

Online scams come in various forms and disguises, aiming to deceive unsuspecting individuals into revealing personal information, providing financial details, or falling for fraudulent schemes. It is vital for parents and educators to educate themselves about the different types of scams prevalent on the internet, such as fake lottery winnings, charity scams, or pyramid schemes, so they can effectively communicate the risks to children and teens. By creating an open dialogue, parents and educators can empower young minds to recognize the red lags associated with scams and to exercise caution when encountering suspicious online offers.

Phishing is another common method used by cybercriminals to trick individuals into divulging sensitive information such as passwords, social security numbers, or credit card details. Parents, educators, schools, and teachers should emphasize the importance of never sharing personal information over email or other forms of online communication unless verified by a trusted source. Teaching children and teens to scrutinize email senders, check for spelling and grammar errors, and avoid clicking on suspicious links can go a long way in preventing falling victim to phishing attempts.

Malware, including viruses, ransomware, and spyware, poses a significant threat to children and teens online. These malicious software can cause damage to devices, compromise personal information, and even lead to identity theft. Parents and educators must educate themselves and stay up-to-date with the latest cybersecurity measures to protect their children and students. Implementing robust antivirus software, regularly updating
operating systems, and teaching safe browsing habits are essential steps in safeguarding against malware attacks.

By understanding the risks associated with online scams, phishing attempts, and malware, parents, educators, schools, and teachers can play a pivotal role in raising cyber- aware kids. Teaching children and teens how to identify and avoid these threats will empower them to navigate the digital landscape safely and responsibly. Together, we can ensure that our children grow up to be resilient and well-prepared individuals in the face of cyber dangers.

TEACHING CHILDREN ABOUT THE DANGERS OF ONLINE GAMING AND VIRTUAL WORLDS

In today's digital age, where children are increasingly connected to the online world, it is vital for parents, educators, schools, and teachers to understand the potential dangers of online gaming and virtual worlds. The virtual realm offers a vast playground of entertainment and social interaction, but it also poses risks that can harm children's well- being and development. To raise cyber-aware kids, we must equip them with the knowledge and skills necessary to navigate these virtual spaces safely.

One of the primary dangers of online gaming and virtual worlds is the potential for cyberbullying. Children may encounter individuals who use the anonymity of the internet to harass, threaten, or intimidate others. It is crucial for parents and educators to teach children how to recognize and respond to cyberbullying, encouraging them to report any inappropriate behavior and providing them with strategies to protect themselves and their peers.

Another concern is the addictive nature of online gaming, which can lead to excessive screen time and neglect of other important aspects of life. Parents and educators should educate children about the potential consequences of excessive gaming, such as poor academic performance, social isolation, and physical health issues. By setting limits on screen time and encouraging a healthy balance between online and ofline activities, we can help children develop a responsible approach to gaming.

Furthermore, children need to be aware of the risks associated with sharing personal information in virtual worlds. It is essential to teach them about the importance of privacy and the potential consequences of sharing sensitive data online. By instilling a sense of caution and emphasizing the need for strong passwords, children can protect themselves from online predators and identity theft.

Additionally, parents and educators should educate children about the distinction between the virtual world and reality. Children need to understand that the friendships and interactions they have online may not always reflect real-life relationships. It is crucial to teach them critical thinking skills and help them develop a healthy skepticism towards online interactions.

By addressing these dangers and teaching children about responsible online behavior, we can empower them to make informed decisions and navigate the digital world safely. Beyond the Screen: Raising Cyber-Aware Kids in a Digital Age provides parents, educators, schools, and teachers with the necessary tools and strategies to equip children with cyber awareness. Together, we can ensure that children and teens thrive in the digital age while minimizing the risks associated with online gaming and virtual worlds.

RECOGNIZING AND REPORTING ONLINE HARASSMENT AND INAPPROPRIATE CONTENT

In today's digital age, it is crucial for parents, educators, schools, and teachers to equip themselves with the knowledge and tools to raise cyber-aware kids. One of the most pressing concerns in this realm is online harassment and exposure to inappropriate content. As our children and teens spend more time online, it becomes increasingly important to recognize the signs of such behavior and empower young individuals to report it promptly.

Online harassment can take many forms, including cyberbullying, hate speech, and even threats of physical harm. It is essential for parents and educators to stay vigilant and educate themselves about the various manifestations of online harassment. By being aware of the warning signs, we can better protect our children and take appropriate action when necessary.

Furthermore, it is crucial to teach our children and teens

about the importance of reporting online harassment and inappropriate content. By fostering an open and supportive environment, we enable them to speak up and seek help if they encounter such situations. Encouraging them to trust their instincts and report any concerning behavior ensures that they do not suffer in silence.

Parents and educators can play a pivotal role by familiarizing themselves with the reporting mechanisms available on different online platforms. It is imperative to know how to report content, block users, and engage with the relevant authorities when needed. By staying informed about these procedures, we can guide our children and teens through the process of reporting and seeking assistance.

Schools and teachers can also contribute significantly to raising cyber-aware kids by incorporating cyber ethics and digital citizenship into their curriculum. By teaching students about responsible online behavior, empathy, and the impact of their words and actions, we can foster a culture of respect and accountability. This approach not only helps prevent online harassment but also empowers students to stand up against inappropriate content and support their peers.

In conclusion, recognizing and reporting online harassment and inappropriate content is a critical aspect of raising cyber-aware kids in a digital age. Parents, educators, schools, and teachers must actively educate themselves about the warning signs, empower children and teens to report such incidents, and provide them with the necessary tools to navigate the online world safely. By working together, we can create a safer and more inclusive digital environment for our children and future generations.

CHAPTER 6: BALANCING SCREEN TIME AND HEALTHY DIGITAL HABITS

Understanding the Impact of Excessive Screen Time on Children's Development

In today's digital age, children are growing up surrounded by screens. From smartphones and tablets to laptops and televisions, screens have become an integral part of their lives.

However, the excessive use of screens can have a detrimental impact on their overall development. In this subchapter, we will delve into the various ways excessive screen time can affect children's development and provide practical strategies for parents, educators, schools, and teachers to raise cyber-aware kids.

One of the most significant impacts of excessive screen time is on children's physical health. Spending hours in front of screens leads to a sedentary lifestyle, contributing to obesity and related health issues. Lack of physical activity not only affects their physical well-being but also hampers their cognitive development. Research suggests that regular exercise stimulates brain growth and enhances children's ability to concentrate, learn, and retain information.

Excessive screen time also interferes with children's social and emotional development. Spending more time interacting with screens and less time engaging in face-to-face interactions hinders the development of essential social skills. Children may struggle with communication, empathy, and building meaningful relationships with their peers.

Additionally, excessive screen time can contribute to increased anxiety, depression, and sleep disturbances in children.

Furthermore, excessive screen time negatively impacts children's cognitive development.
Constant exposure to screens can lead to attention deficits, decreased memory, and reduced problem-solving skills. The constant barrage of information and stimuli from screens also hampers their ability to focus and concentrate on tasks. This can have a significant impact on their academic performance and overall learning abilities.

To counteract the negative impact of excessive screen time, parents, educators, schools, and teachers must work together to raise cyber-aware kids. Setting limits on screen time, encouraging physical activity, and promoting face-to-face interactions are crucial steps. Additionally, incorporating digital literacy programs in schools and educating children about online safety, privacy, and responsible digital citizenship can empower them to navigate the digital world responsibly.

By understanding the impact of excessive screen time on children's development and implementing practical strategies, parents, educators, schools, and teachers can ensure that children grow up to be well-rounded individuals in the digital age. Together, we can create a generation of cyber-aware kids who can thrive in both the virtual and real world.

PROMOTING PHYSICAL ACTIVITY AND OFFLINE INTERESTS

In today's digital age, it's crucial for parents, educators, schools, and teachers to understand the importance of promoting physical activity and ofline interests among children and teens. As technology continues to advance and screen time becomes increasingly prevalent, it is becoming more challenging to encourage kids to engage in physical activities and explore ofline hobbies. However, by addressing this issue head-on and implementing effective strategies, we can help our children lead healthier, well-rounded lives.

Regular physical activity is essential for a child's development, both physically and mentally. It boosts their cardiovascular health, strengthens their muscles and bones, and improves their overall fitness. Moreover, engaging in physical activities helps children develop important life skills such as teamwork, discipline, and resilience. As cyber awareness for children and teens becomes a priority, it is crucial to remember that physical activity is equally important in their overall well-being.

Encouraging physical activity can be achieved through various means. Parents and educators can promote active lifestyles by organizing outdoor playdates, participating in sports clubs, or scheduling regular family walks or bike rides. Schools and teachers can incorporate physical education classes, recess breaks, and extracurricular activities that focus on movement and exercise. By creating an environment that supports and values physical activity, we can instill healthy habits in our children from an early age.

Furthermore, it is equally important to foster ofline interests among children and teens. Encouraging them to explore hobbies such as reading, painting, playing a musical instrument, or engaging in outdoor activities not only helps them develop new skills but also provides a healthy balance to their screen time. Ofline interests provide opportunities for personal growth, creativity, and self- expression, enabling children to discover their passions and talents outside the digital realm.

Parents, educators, schools, and teachers play a crucial role in promoting physical activity and ofline interests among children and teens. By setting a positive example and actively participating in these activities ourselves, we can inspire our children to follow suit.

Additionally, open communication and collaboration between parents and schools are essential to ensure that children are receiving a well-rounded education that includes not only cyber awareness but also physical and ofline engagement.

In conclusion, promoting physical activity and ofline interests in today's digital age is paramount for the holistic development of children and teens. By prioritizing these aspects, we can raise cyber-aware kids who are not only technologically savvy but also physically active, mentally resilient, and creatively fulfilled individuals. Let us work together to strike a healthy balance between the digital and ofline worlds, providing our children with a well-rounded upbringing that prepares them for success in the digital age and beyond.

CREATING A HEALTHY FAMILY MEDIA PLAN

In today's digital age, it is essential for parents, educators, and schools to prioritize cyber awareness for children and teens. With the omnipresence of screens and devices, it is crucial to establish a healthy family media plan to ensure that children are equipped with the necessary skills to navigate the digital world responsibly. This subchapter aims to provide practical guidance on creating such a plan, empowering parents and educators to raise cyber-aware kids.

1.   Set Clear Boundaries: Begin by establishing clear boundaries for screen time. Determine the appropriate duration and frequency of device usage for your child based on their age, developmental stage, and individual needs. Communicate these boundaries effectively, ensuring that everyone in the family understands and respects them.

2. Lead by Example: Children often imitate their parents' behavior. Be a positive role model by demonstrating responsible tech use. Limit your own screen time, engage
in meaningful ofline activities, and prioritize face-to-face interactions. This not only fosters
healthy habits but also encourages open conversations about the benefits and risks of technology.

3. Encourage Balance: Encourage a balanced lifestyle that

includes a variety of activities beyond screens. Promote physical activities, hobbies, reading, and social engagements to help children develop well-rounded personalities and reduce excessive reliance on technology.

4. Establish Tech-Free Zones and Times: Designate specific areas in your home where screens are not allowed, such as bedrooms or dining areas. Additionally, establish tech-free times, such as during meals or before bedtime, to encourage quality family time and promote healthy sleep habits.

5. Foster Digital Literacy: Teach children about responsible online behavior, including privacy, security, and ethical considerations. Educate them about the dangers of cyberbullying, online predators, and the importance of maintaining a positive digital footprint. Encourage critical thinking and discernment when consuming online content.

6. Emphasize Open Communication: Create an environment where children feel comfortable discussing their online experiences, concerns, and questions. Encourage open communication by actively listening, expressing empathy, and providing guidance when needed. Regularly check in with your child's online activities and discuss any potential risks or issues.

By implementing a healthy family media plan, parents, educators, and schools can equip children with the necessary skills and knowledge to navigate the digital world safely and responsibly. This subchapter provides a comprehensive guide to help families create a balanced and cyber-aware environment, fostering the growth and development of children and teens in the digital age.

CHAPTER 7: STAYING UP-TO- DATE WITH TECHNOLOGY

Keeping Yourself Informed about the Latest Digital Trends and Apps

In today's digital age, it is crucial for parents, educators, schools, and teachers to stay informed about the latest digital trends and apps. As the world becomes increasingly interconnected and technology continues to evolve at a rapid pace, it is essential to equip ourselves with the knowledge to effectively guide and protect our children and students. This subchapter aims to provide valuable insights and strategies to enhance cyber awareness for children and teens.

With new digital trends and apps emerging regularly, it can be challenging to keep up. However, by staying informed, we can better understand the potential risks and benefits associated with these technologies. By actively engaging in ongoing learning, we can ensure that we are equipped to have meaningful conversations with children and teens about their digital lives.

One effective way to stay informed is by regularly attending workshops, conferences, or webinars focused on cyber awareness. These events often feature experts who provide valuable insights into the latest digital trends and apps. Additionally, subscribing to reputable online resources, such as blogs or newsletters, can help us remain up-to-date with the ever-changing digital landscape.

Furthermore, engaging with other parents, educators, schools, and teachers can be a valuable source of information. Joining online communities or attending local meetups can provide opportunities to share experiences, discuss challenges, and exchange knowledge on the latest digital trends. Collaborating with others in our network can help us stay ahead of potential risks and ensure we are providing accurate guidance to children and teens.

Another essential aspect of staying informed is maintaining open lines of communication with children and teens. Regularly engaging in conversations about their digital experiences can provide valuable insights into the platforms and apps they are using. By actively listening and asking questions, we can gain a deeper understanding of their digital lives and address any concerns or potential risks that may arise.

In conclusion, keeping ourselves informed about the latest digital trends and apps is crucial in raising cyber-aware kids in a digital age. By actively seeking knowledge, engaging with others, and maintaining open communication with children and teens, we can effectively navigate the ever-changing digital landscape. Together, as parents, educators, schools, and teachers, we can empower the next generation to make informed decisions and stay safe online.

LEARNING AND EXPLORING TECHNOLOGY TOGETHER WITH YOUR CHILD

In this digital age, it is crucial for parents, educators, schools, and teachers to guide children in developing cyber awareness. By teaching them to navigate the online world responsibly, we can empower them to make informed choices and stay safe. One effective way to achieve this is by learning and exploring technology together with your child.

Technology is an integral part of our lives, and it is essential for parents and educators to stay up-to-date with the latest trends and platforms. By actively engaging with technology, you can better understand the potential risks and opportunities it presents.
This knowledge will enable you to guide your child effectively and answer any questions they may have.

When learning and exploring technology together, it is important to create a safe and non-judgmental environment. Encourage open discussions with your child, allowing them to share their experiences and concerns. By actively listening and engaging in conversation, you can address any misconceptions or fears they may have about technology.

Take advantage of teachable moments. Whether it's setting up parental controls on devices, discussing the importance of strong passwords, or exploring privacy settings on social media platforms, these moments provide valuable opportunities for learning. By involving your child in these processes, they will develop the necessary skills to protect themselves online.

Additionally, consider integrating technology into educational activities. Explore age- appropriate websites, apps, and games that encourage learning and critical thinking. This not only fosters a positive relationship with technology but also enhances your child's digital literacy skills.

Collaborative projects are another effective way to learn and explore technology together. Encourage your child to brainstorm ideas for creative projects that utilize digital tools, such as creating a website, designing a digital poster, or coding a simple game. By working together, you can foster a sense of teamwork and empower your child to become a responsible digital citizen.

Remember, learning and exploring technology together should be an ongoing process. Stay curious, keep learning, and adapt as technology evolves. By actively participating in your child's technological journey, you can instill the necessary skills and values they need to navigate the digital landscape safely and confidently.

ADAPTING TO THE EVER-EVOLVING DIGITAL LANDSCAPE

As parents, educators, schools, and teachers, it is our responsibility to guide and protect children and teens in the ever-evolving digital landscape. With technology constantly advancing, it is crucial to stay informed and adapt our approaches to ensure cyber awareness for the younger generation.

In this subchapter, we will explore various strategies and techniques to help our children and teens navigate the digital world safely and responsibly. By empowering them with the necessary knowledge and skills, we can equip them to make informed decisions online and protect their digital identities.

One of the key aspects of adapting to the digital landscape is staying up-to-date with the latest trends and technologies. This includes understanding popular social media platforms, online gaming communities, and messaging apps. By familiarizing ourselves with these platforms, we can have meaningful conversations with our children and provide guidance on potential risks and responsible usage.

Another essential factor in adapting to the digital landscape is educating ourselves about the potential dangers and threats that exist online. From cyberbullying to phishing scams, it is crucial to be aware of these risks and teach our children how to recognize and respond to them. By fostering open communication with our children, we can create a safe space for them to discuss any concerns or incidents they encounter online.

Additionally, it is important to establish clear rules and guidelines for online behavior. This includes setting boundaries on screen time, teaching children about the importance of privacy settings, and emphasizing the significance of treating others with respect and kindness online. By establishing these guidelines, we can help children develop healthy digital habits and protect them from potential harm.

Furthermore, it is vital to educate children and teens about the long-term consequences of their digital actions. From sharing personal information to posting inappropriate content, we must emphasize the potential impact on their reputation and future opportunities. By teaching them about digital footprints, online privacy, and the permanence of online content, we can empower them to think before they act and make responsible choices.

In conclusion, adapting to the ever-evolving digital landscape is essential for parents, educators, schools, and teachers invested in raising cyber-aware kids. By staying informed, educating ourselves and our children about online risks, setting clear guidelines, and fostering open communication, we can create a safer digital environment for the younger generation. Together, we can equip children and teens with the necessary skills and knowledge to navigate the digital world responsibly, ensuring their safety and well- being in this rapidly changing digital age.

CHAPTER 8: COLLABORATING WITH SCHOOLS AND EDUCATORS

Establishing Partnerships with Schools to Promote Cyber Awareness

In today's digital age, where children and teens are increasingly exposed to the online world, it is essential for parents, educators, and schools to work together to raise cyber-aware kids. By establishing partnerships with schools, we can create a comprehensive approach to educating children about online safety, privacy, and responsible digital citizenship. This subchapter will explore the benefits of such partnerships and provide practical strategies for implementing them.

One of the most significant advantages of partnering with schools is the access to a larger audience. Schools serve as a central hub for children and teenagers, providing an ideal platform to disseminate cyber awareness information effectively. By collaborating with educators and schools, parents can leverage their expertise and resources to create a more impactful learning experience for students.

To establish successful partnerships, it is crucial for parents and schools to communicate openly and regularly. Hosting regular meetings, workshops, or seminars can facilitate discussions between parents, educators, and schools, fostering a supportive network where all stakeholders can share their insights, concerns, and experiences related to cyber awareness. These forums also provide an opportunity to invite experts in the field to address specific concerns and provide guidance on the latest trends and challenges in online safety.

Schools can also play a pivotal role in integrating cyber awareness education into their curriculum. By including dedicated lessons or modules on digital literacy and online safety, schools can ensure that all students receive consistent and age- appropriate cyber awareness education. This collaboration between parents and schools will reinforce the importance of digital safety and provide students with the necessary skills to navigate the online world responsibly.

Furthermore, partnerships with schools can extend beyond the classroom. By organizing joint initiatives such as cyber awareness campaigns, parents and educators can engage the entire school community in promoting safe online practices. This can involve organizing events, competitions, or awareness drives that encourage students to actively participate in discussions, share their experiences, and learn from one another.

In conclusion, establishing partnerships with schools is an essential step in raising cyber- aware kids. By combining the efforts of parents, educators, and schools, we can create a comprehensive approach to cyber awareness education. Through open communication, integrating cyber awareness into the curriculum, and organizing joint initiatives, we can empower children and teens with the necessary knowledge and skills to navigate the digital world safely and responsibly. Together, we can create a generation of digitally literate individuals who are equipped to thrive in the digital age.

SUPPORTING TEACHERS IN INTEGRATING DIGITAL LITERACY INTO THE CURRICULUM

In today's digital age, it is crucial for educators to equip students with the necessary skills to navigate the online world safely and responsibly. Digital literacy has become an essential component of the curriculum, and it is vital that teachers receive the support they need to effectively integrate it into their teaching practices.

Parents, educators, schools, and teachers all play a pivotal role in ensuring that children and teens develop cyber awareness skills. By working together, we can create a safe and secure online environment for young learners.

One of the first steps in supporting teachers is providing them with professional development opportunities. Many educators may feel overwhelmed or unsure about how to incorporate digital literacy into their lessons. By offering workshops and training sessions specifically focused on digital literacy, teachers can gain the knowledge and skills they need to confidently address this important topic in their classrooms.

Additionally, schools should provide teachers with access to resources and tools that promote digital literacy. This may include educational apps, online platforms, or websites that offer age-appropriate content related to cyber awareness. By having access to these resources, teachers can easily integrate digital literacy into their lesson plans and engage students in meaningful discussions about online safety, privacy, and responsible digital citizenship.

It is also essential for parents to be involved in supporting teachers in integrating digital literacy into the curriculum. Parents can reinforce the lessons taught in the classroom by emphasizing the importance of online safety and setting clear boundaries for internet use at home. Schools can organize parent workshops to educate them about digital literacy and provide tips on how to monitor their children's online activities effectively.

Collaboration between educators, schools, and parents is key to ensuring that digital literacy becomes an integral part of the curriculum. By working together, we can create a comprehensive approach to cyber awareness that empowers children and teens to make informed decisions online.

In conclusion, supporting teachers in integrating digital literacy into the curriculum is crucial for raising cyber-aware kids in a digital age. Providing professional development opportunities, access to resources, and fostering collaboration between educators and parents are all essential steps in creating a safe and secure online environment for our children. By prioritizing digital literacy, we can equip young learners with the skills they need to navigate the digital world responsibly and become responsible digital citizens.

ORGANIZING PARENT WORKSHOPS AND EDUCATIONAL PROGRAMS

In today's digital age, where technology is an integral part of our daily lives, it is crucial for parents, educators, schools, and teachers to come together to raise cyber-aware kids. As children and teens navigate the online world, it is imperative that they are equipped with the necessary knowledge and skills to stay safe and make responsible choices. One effective way to achieve this is through organizing parent workshops and educational programs.

Parent workshops serve as a platform for parents to learn about the latest digital trends, potential risks, and strategies to foster a safe online environment for their children. These workshops can be conducted in schools, community centers, or even online, allowing parents to attend at their convenience. By addressing the concerns and challenges faced by parents in the digital realm, these workshops empower them to guide their children effectively.

Educational programs, on the other hand, focus on equipping educators, schools, and teachers with the tools and resources needed to promote cyber awareness among children and teens.

These programs can cover a wide range of topics, including internet safety, social media etiquette, online privacy, digital footprints, and responsible digital citizenship. By enhancing the digital literacy of educators, they can effectively educate and guide their students towards responsible online behavior.

When organizing parent workshops and educational programs, it is crucial to collaborate with experts in the field of cyber awareness. Inviting guest speakers, such as cybersecurity professionals, child psychologists, or law enforcement officers, can provide valuable insights and guidance.

Additionally, incorporating interactive activities, role-playing scenarios, and real-life case studies can make the workshops and programs engaging and impactful.

To ensure maximum participation and engagement, it is essential to promote these workshops and programs extensively. Utilize various channels, such as school newsletters, social media platforms, and parent-teacher associations, to spread the word. Consider offering incentives, such as certificates of participation or free resources, to encourage parents and educators to attend.

By organizing parent workshops and educational programs focused on cyber awareness, parents, educators, schools, and teachers can come together to create a safer and more responsible digital environment for children and teens. These initiatives not only equip parents with the necessary knowledge but also empower educators to guide their students effectively. Together, we can raise a generation of cyber-aware kids who navigate the digital world with confidence and responsibility.

CHAPTER 9: MANAGING ONLINE CHALLENGES AND CRISIS SITUATIONS

Dealing with Cyberbullying Incidents and Supporting Victims

In today's digital age, where children and teenagers spend a significant amount of their time online, it is crucial for parents, educators, schools, and teachers to address the issue of cyberbullying. Cyberbullying refers to the act of using technology, such as social media platforms, text messages, or emails, to harass, intimidate, or harm others. As adults responsible for the well-being of children, it is our duty to equip them with the necessary tools to navigate the online world safely.

When it comes to dealing with cyberbullying incidents, the first step is to recognize the signs. Changes in behavior, sudden withdrawal from social activities, or a decline in academic performance may indicate that a child is experiencing cyberbullying. It is important to create an open and non-judgmental environment where children feel comfortable discussing their online experiences.

Once a cyberbullying incident is identified, it is crucial to take immediate action. This involves documenting the evidence, such as screenshots or saved messages, and reporting the incident to the appropriate platform or website. Most social media platforms have mechanisms in place to report and block users engaging in cyberbullying. Additionally, parents and teachers should inform school administrators, who can take disciplinary action if necessary.

Supporting the victims of cyberbullying is equally important. Victims often experience emotional distress, anxiety, and a decline in self-esteem. It is crucial for parents and educators to provide a supportive network and encourage open communication. It may be helpful to involve a counselor or therapist who can guide the child through the healing process.

Educating children about cyber awareness is a proactive approach to preventing cyberbullying. Parents, educators, schools, and teachers should teach children how to protect their personal information, how to identify and report cyberbullying, and the importance of responsible online behavior. Implementing digital citizenship programs and integrating cyber awareness into the curriculum can help children develop the necessary skills to navigate the online world safely.

In conclusion, dealing with cyberbullying incidents and supporting victims requires a collaborative effort from parents, educators, schools, and teachers. By recognizing the signs, taking immediate action, and providing a supportive environment, we can help victims heal and prevent future incidents. Educating children about cyber awareness is the key to raising cyber-aware kids who can navigate the digital age confidently and safely.

RESPONDING TO ONLINE THREATS, HARASSMENT, AND IMPERSONATION

In today's digital age, it is crucial for parents, educators, schools, and teachers to equip themselves with the knowledge and strategies to help children and teens navigate the online world safely. One of the significant challenges that young individuals face online is dealing with threats, harassment, and impersonation. This subchapter aims to provide practical guidance on how to respond effectively to these issues and protect our children's digital well-being.

Online threats can take various forms, such as cyberbullying, hate speech, or even predators seeking to exploit vulnerable individuals.
Recognizing the signs of online threats is essential for parents and educators to intervene promptly. The chapter will delve into the warning signs to look out for, including sudden changes in behavior, withdrawal from social activities, or reluctance to use digital devices. It will emphasize the importance of open communication with children and teens, creating a safe and non-judgmental environment where they feel comfortable discussing their online experiences.

Once an online threat is identified, it is crucial to take immediate action. This subchapter will provide step-by-step guidance on how to document and report incidents to the relevant authorities, whether it be the school administration, social media platform, or law enforcement agencies. Additionally, it will explore various strategies to support the affected child or teen, such as seeking professional help, involving school counselors, or engaging in online support communities.

Harassment, both online and ofline, can have severe psychological and emotional consequences. This subchapter will shed light on the importance of teaching children and teens about empathy, respect, and responsible digital citizenship. It will provide practical tips on how to respond to online harassers, including blocking and reporting abusive individuals, as well as strategies to strengthen resilience and self-esteem.

Impersonation is another growing concern in the digital world. This subchapter will highlight the risks associated with impersonation, such as identity theft or reputation damage, and provide guidance on preventive measures, such as safeguarding personal information and using privacy settings. It will also offer advice on how to respond if impersonation occurs, including reporting the incident, documenting evidence, and seeking legal assistance if necessary.

In conclusion, this subchapter on responding to online threats, harassment, and impersonation aims to empower parents, educators, schools, and teachers with the necessary tools to protect children and teens in the digital age. By fostering open communication, promoting empathy, and providing practical strategies, we can raise cyber-aware kids who can navigate the online world confidently and safely.

Seeking Professional Help and Resources for Online Addiction and Mental Health Issues

Seeking Professional Help and Resources for Online Addiction and Mental Health Issues
In today's digital age, where children and teens are increasingly immersed in the online world, it is crucial for parents, educators, and schools to be aware of the potential risks and challenges that come with excessive screen time. One of the most pressing concerns is online addiction and its impact on mental health. Recognizing the signs and seeking professional help and resources is essential in addressing these issues effectively.

Online addiction is a growing phenomenon that can have severe consequences on a child or teen's well-being. Excessive use of the internet, social media platforms, and online gaming can lead to a range of mental health problems such as anxiety, depression, and social isolation. It is crucial for parents and educators to remain vigilant and proactive in identifying signs of addiction, including withdrawal from ofline activities, neglecting responsibilities, and a preoccupation with online activities.

When it comes to seeking professional help, there are several avenues to consider. First and foremost, parents should consult with their child's pediatrician or a mental health professional who specializes in internet addiction and related issues. These professionals can provide guidance, conduct assessments, and recommend appropriate treatment options tailored to the child's needs.

In addition to individual therapy, support groups and counseling services specifically designed for online addiction can be immensely helpful. These resources provide a safe and understanding environment where children and teens can share their experiences, learn coping strategies, and receive guidance from peers who have faced similar challenges. Many schools and community organizations offer such support groups, making it easier for parents and educators to connect their children with these valuable resources.

It is also important for parents, educators, and schools to educate themselves about cyber awareness and mental health issues. By staying informed, they can better understand the challenges their children face and provide appropriate support. There are numerous online resources, books, and workshops available that provide valuable insights into online addiction, gaming disorders, and mental health concerns related to excessive screen time.

In conclusion, seeking professional help and resources for online addiction and mental health issues is essential for parents, educators, and schools in raising cyber-aware kids. By recognizing the signs, consulting with professionals, and utilizing available resources, we can effectively address these challenges and ensure the well-being of our children in the digital age. Together, we can empower our children to navigate the online world responsibly, while fostering their mental health and overall well-being.

CHAPTER 10: EMPOWERING CHILDREN TO BE CYBER ADVOCATES

Encouraging Children to Be Upstanders and Digital Leaders

In today's digital age, it is crucial for parents, educators, schools, and teachers to equip children with the skills and knowledge to navigate the online world responsibly. Cyber awareness for children and teens is a pressing concern, as they are increasingly exposed to various online risks and challenges. One of the most effective ways to address these issues is by encouraging children to become upstanders and digital leaders.

An upstander is someone who stands up against bullying, harassment, or any form of negativity online. By fostering a culture of empathy, respect, and inclusivity, parents and educators can empower children to take a stand against cyberbullying and other harmful behaviors. Teaching children the importance of empathy and kindness will not only help them become responsible digital citizens but also contribute to creating a safer online environment for everyone.

Becoming a digital leader goes beyond being a passive user of technology. It involves actively engaging with digital platforms, promoting positive content, and using technology to make a difference. Parents and educators can inspire children to become digital leaders by encouraging them to share their knowledge and skills with others. This can be done through mentoring programs or by involving children in online safety initiatives within their schools or communities.

Furthermore, it is essential to teach children critical thinking skills and media literacy. With the vast amount of information available online, children need to learn how to evaluate the credibility and reliability of sources. By developing their critical thinking abilities, children can discern between trustworthy and misleading information, thus minimizing the risk of falling victim to scams, misinformation, or online predators.

Parents, educators, schools, and teachers should also emphasize the significance of digital footprints and responsible online behavior. Children need to understand that their actions online can have long-lasting consequences. By teaching them about privacy settings, the importance of strong passwords, and the potential dangers of oversharing personal information, we can help children protect themselves and their digital identities.

In conclusion, the subchapter "Encouraging Children to Be Upstanders and Digital Leaders" is dedicated to guiding parents, educators, schools, and teachers in instilling cyber awareness for children and teens. By fostering empathy, promoting critical thinking, and emphasizing responsible online behavior, we can raise a generation of digital leaders who actively contribute to a safer and more positive online environment.

TEACHING RESPONSIBLE ONLINE ACTIVISM AND SOCIAL ADVOCACY

In today's digital age, children and teens are more connected than ever before. They have a world of information and resources at their fingertips, allowing them to become active participants in shaping the world around them. However, with this power comes the responsibility to use it wisely and ethically. As parents, educators, schools, and teachers, it is crucial to guide and teach our young ones about responsible online activism and social advocacy.

Responsible online activism involves using digital platforms to bring attention to important social issues and promote positive change. It empowers young people to stand up for what they believe in and make a difference. However, it is vital to teach them that activism should be conducted in a respectful and responsible manner.

One essential aspect of teaching responsible online activism is helping children and teens understand the potential impact of their actions. They should learn to critically evaluate the information they come across and verify its authenticity before sharing it with others. Encouraging them to fact-check, use reliable sources, and consider multiple perspectives will help them become discerning digital citizens.

Moreover, children and teens need to understand the importance of respectful and inclusive communication. Online platforms often expose them to diverse opinions and beliefs. Teaching them how to engage in constructive conversations, listen actively, and express their views respectfully is paramount. By promoting empathy and understanding, we can foster healthy debates and discourage cyberbullying or hate speech.

Social advocacy is another crucial component that should be addressed. Children and teens should be encouraged to identify and support causes they are passionate about. Educators and parents can guide them in researching organizations or charities that align with their interests and values. Teaching them how to use social media platforms effectively to raise awareness, fundraise, or organize events will empower them to become active agents of change.

In conclusion, teaching responsible online activism and social advocacy to children and teens is essential in today's digital age. By equipping them with the necessary skills to navigate the online world responsibly and ethically, we can empower them to make a positive impact on society. As parents, educators, schools, and teachers, it is our collective responsibility to guide them, promote critical thinking, empathy, and respectful communication. Together, we can raise cyber-aware kids who are not only digitally savvy but also socially conscious and actively engaged in creating a better world.

FOSTERING A CULTURE OF EMPATHY, KINDNESS, AND RESPECT IN THE DIGITAL WORLD

In today's digital age, where children and teens are constantly connected to technology, it is crucial for parents, educators, schools, and teachers to focus on fostering a culture of empathy, kindness, and respect in the online world. As cyber awareness for children and teens becomes increasingly important, it is our responsibility to guide them towards becoming responsible digital citizens who understand the importance of treating others with empathy and respect in the digital sphere.

Empathy is a fundamental aspect of human interaction, and it should not be left behind when we enter the digital realm. Teaching our children and teens how to empathize with others, even online, is essential. Encourage them to think about how their words and actions might impact others emotionally. By fostering empathy, we can help them develop a sense of responsibility for their online behavior, ensuring that they contribute positively to the digital world.

Kindness is another crucial value that needs to be emphasized in the digital landscape.

Encourage your children and students to use their online presence to spread kindness and positivity. Remind them that even a small act of kindness, such as sending an uplifting message or complimenting someone's work, can brighten someone's day. By focusing on kindness, we can create a supportive and inclusive environment online.

Respect is the foundation of healthy relationships, both online and ofline. Teach your children and teens the importance of treating others with respect, regardless of their differences or opinions. Encourage them to engage in respectful conversations and to be open-minded when encountering different perspectives. By practicing respectful behavior online, we can create a safe and inclusive digital space for everyone.

To foster a culture of empathy, kindness, and respect in the digital world, it is important to lead by example. As parents, educators, schools, and teachers, we must demonstrate these values in our own online interactions. Engage in positive conversations, demonstrate empathy towards others, and always treat others with respect. Our actions will serve as powerful examples for the younger generation to follow.

In conclusion, fostering a culture of empathy, kindness, and respect in the digital world is crucial for the development of responsible digital citizens. By emphasizing these values, we can create a supportive and inclusive online environment where children and teens can thrive. Let us work together to raise cyber-aware kids who understand the importance of empathy, kindness, and respect in the digital age.

CHAPTER 11: CONCLUSION

Reflecting on the Journey of Raising Cyber- Aware Kids

As parents, educators, and teachers, we have embarked on a remarkable journey - raising cyber-aware kids in a digital age. Our children, born into a world filled with screens, gadgets, and the vast expanse of the internet, face unique challenges and opportunities. It is our responsibility to guide them through this ever-evolving digital landscape, ensuring their safety, well-being, and ability to thrive in a technologically driven society.

Reflecting on this journey, we can't help but marvel at how far we've come. We have witnessed our children grow from curious toddlers who could barely navigate a touchscreen to tech-savvy teenagers who effortlessly navigate the internet. Along the way, we have confronted numerous challenges, faced unforeseen dangers, and celebrated countless victories.

One of the most critical aspects of raising cyber-aware kids is fostering open communication. As parents, we have learned the importance of having honest conversations about the potential risks and benefits of the digital world. We have created safe spaces where our children can come to us with their questions, concerns, and experiences. Through these discussions, we have developed a deep understanding of the online world and the impact it has on our children's lives.

We have also discovered the power of education in shaping our children's digital literacy. As educators and teachers, we have incorporated cyber awareness into our classrooms, teaching children how to navigate the internet responsibly, distinguish between reliable and misleading information, and protect their personal data. We have witnessed the transformation of our students into responsible digital citizens, equipped with the knowledge and skills to make informed decisions online.

Throughout this journey, we have come to realize that raising cyber-aware kids is not just about protection and restriction. It is about empowering our children to make wise choices, encouraging them to explore the digital world safely, and nurturing their critical thinking skills. It is about teaching them to be proactive rather than reactive, to be creators rather than consumers, and to use technology as a tool for growth and self-expression.

As we reflect on this journey, we acknowledge that our work is far from over. The digital landscape continues to evolve, presenting new challenges and opportunities. However, armed with knowledge, communication, and a deep understanding of our children's needs, we are confident in our ability to raise cyber-aware kids who can thrive in a digital age.

Together, let us continue this journey, supporting and guiding one another as we navigate the ever-changing world of technology and empower the next generation to become responsible, resilient, and cyber- aware individuals.

EMBRACING THE OPPORTUNITIES AND BENEFITS OF THE DIGITAL AGE

In today's fast-paced world, the digital age has become an integral part of our lives. With technology advancing at an unprecedented rate, it is crucial for parents, educators, schools, and teachers to understand the opportunities and benefits that the digital age offers, especially when it comes to cyber awareness for children and teens.

The digital age has revolutionized the way we learn, communicate, and access information. With the click of a button, we can connect with people across the globe, explore diverse cultures, and gain knowledge that was once confined to textbooks. This vast pool of information is a valuable resource that can greatly enhance a child's education. By embracing the digital age, parents and educators have the opportunity to expose children to a wealth of knowledge and foster their curiosity, leading to a more engaged and informed generation.

Furthermore, the digital age provides a platform for creativity and self-expression. Children and teens can explore their interests, share their unique talents, and connect with like-minded individuals through various online communities. From creating digital art to coding their own video games, the digital age empowers young minds to unleash their imagination and pursue their passions. By embracing these opportunities, parents and educators can help foster a sense of purpose and fulfillment in children, building their confidence and self-esteem.

Moreover, the digital age offers numerous practical benefits. Online learning platforms enable students to access educational resources at their own convenience, promoting self-paced learning and personalized education. In addition, digital tools and applications can help streamline administrative tasks for educators, allowing them to focus more on engaging with students and delivering quality education.

However, it is vital to approach the digital age with caution and ensure cyber awareness among children and teens. With the ever- evolving online landscape, children need to be equipped with the knowledge and skills to navigate the digital world safely. Parents, educators, schools, and teachers must collaborate to educate children about the potential risks of the internet, such as cyberbullying, online predators, and identity theft. By teaching them about responsible digital citizenship, we can empower children to make informed decisions and protect themselves in the online realm.

In conclusion, embracing the opportunities and benefits of the digital age is essential for parents, educators, schools, and teachers invested in cyber awareness for children and teens. By utilizing technology as a tool for education, creativity, and self-expression, we can equip the younger generation with the skills and knowledge they need to thrive in the digital era. However, it is equally important to prioritize cyber awareness and ensure children have the necessary tools to navigate the online world safely. By striking a balance between embracing the digital age and promoting responsible digital citizenship, we can raise cyber-aware kids who are prepared for the challenges and opportunities of the digital age.

CONTINUING THE CONVERSATION AND STAYING COMMITTED TO CYBER AWARENESS

In this fast-paced digital age, it is crucial for parents, educators, schools, and teachers to continue the conversation and stay committed to raising cyber-aware kids. The ever-evolving landscape of the internet presents both opportunities and challenges for children and teens, making it imperative for us to equip them with the necessary tools and knowledge to navigate the online world safely.

One of the key aspects of continuing the conversation about cyber awareness is open communication. It is vital for parents and educators to maintain an ongoing dialogue with children and teens about their online experiences. By fostering a non-judgmental and supportive environment, we can encourage them to share any concerns, questions, or incidents they encounter online. This open dialogue will not only help us understand their digital lives better but also enable us to provide guidance and support whenever needed.

Staying committed to cyber awareness involves staying up-to-date with the latest trends, technologies, and risks in the digital world. As responsible adults, we must educate ourselves about the various platforms, apps, and social media sites that children and teens are using. By gaining knowledge about their online habits, we can identify potential risks and take preventive measures to ensure their online safety.

Furthermore, it is essential to educate children and teens about responsible digital citizenship. Teaching them about the importance of privacy, respecting others' boundaries, and being mindful of their online behavior will empower them to make informed decisions and create a positive online presence. Encouraging empathy and kindness in their online interactions will foster a healthy digital community and protect them from cyberbullying or online harassment.

In addition to these proactive measures, it is crucial to establish clear rules and boundaries for internet usage. Setting age-appropriate limits on screen time, monitoring their online activities, and implementing parental controls can help mitigate potential risks. It is equally important to teach children about the importance of ofline activities, such as spending time with family and friends, engaging in hobbies, and maintaining a healthy balance between online and ofline life.

Finally, collaboration between parents, educators, schools, and teachers is vital in ensuring the effectiveness of cyber awareness efforts. Regular meetings, workshops, and training sessions can help share best practices, exchange ideas, and address any challenges faced in raising cyber-aware kids.

By continuing the conversation and staying committed to cyber awareness, we can empower our children and teens to make responsible choices, navigate the digital world safely, and become confident digital citizens. Together, let's create a generation that embraces technology while understanding its potential risks and ensuring a safer online environment for all.

MARK HUGHES

Mark Hughes retired from a career in law enforcement after having served for over 25 years. He started out as a campus police officer with the University of South Alabama, as a Reserve Officer with The City of Mobile, Alabama, then on to the Birmingham Alabama Police Department. In 1998 he moved to Washington, DC and having been tinkering around and building his own computers, got a job with a Washington National Cathedral School, the St. Alban's School for Boys. Here he worked his way up from the help desk to the network administrator in just 3 years. He left St. Albans after six years and ended back in Alabama.

Mark went back into law enforcement with the Jefferson County Sheriff's Office and then on to the Shelby County's Sheriff's Office. Mark was a patrol deputy for five years and then became the first patrol deputy evidence technician. He moved into Investigations shortly afterwards where he spent time as the evidence custodian and evidence technician and then as an Investigator. Mark investigated every type crime there was but after going to classes with the National Computer Forensics Institute he found his niche as a computer/cell phone forensics examiner. He was sworn in as a deputy US Marshall to work federal cases with the US Secret Service Electronic Crimes Task Force which he served on for three years. These schools and his network administration knowledge is where he learned most of his knowledge about cybercrime and the dangers posed to kids by the digital age. He forensically examined most every piece of evidence involved in child exploitation cases and child pornography cases that came through the Sheriff's Office and worked hundreds of pieces of evidence that came through the USSS Electronics Crimes Task Force.

Mark currently lives in Hoover, Alabama with his wife and three dogs.

CYBER KIDS

A guide to understanding the dangers of the Internet and how to keep your kids safe while maintaining the good of the Internet.

www.ingramcontent.com/pod-product-compliance
Lightning Source LLC
LaVergne TN
LVHW051747050326
832903LV00029B/2765